NOV 13

# Ripley's Believe It or Not!

**Developed and produced by Ripley Publishing Ltd**

This edition published and distributed by:

Mason Crest
450 Parkway Drive, Suite D, Broomall, PA 19008
www.masoncrest.com

Printed and bound in the United States of America

First printing
9 8 7 6 5 4 3 2 1

Ripley's Believe It or Not!
Crazy World
ISBN: 978-1-4222-2776-3 (hardback)
ISBN: 978-1-4222-9037-8 (e-book)
Ripley's Believe It or Not!–Complete 8 Title Series
ISBN: 978-1-4222-2979-8

Cataloging-in-Publication Data on file with the Library of Congress

PUBLISHER'S NOTE
While every effort has been made to verify the accuracy of the entries in this book, the
Publishers cannot be held responsible for any errors contained in the work. They would
be glad to receive any information from readers.

WARNING
Some of the stunts and activities in this book are undertaken by experts and should not
be attempted by anyone without adequate training and supervision.

# Ripley's Believe It or Not!®

## Strikingly True

# CRAZY WORLD

www.MasonCrest.com

# CRAZY WORLD

Find out about our amazing world! Discover the

sensational world we live in. Take a look at the

70-ft (20-m) sandstorm that hit central China,

the bright pink salt lake in Senegal, and the tiny

6-ft-wide (1.8-m) house in Wales.

*This extraordinary house is made out of*
*43,000 plastic beer crates...*

**Ripley's Believe It or Not!®**

# March OF THE Lava

The active volcano of Kilauea in Hawaii has been constantly erupting since 1983, and its unstoppable flow of burning lava has devastated hundreds of homes and businesses in its vicinity. Incredibly, it has also gradually extended Hawaii's coastline by an area the size of Washington, D.C.

In 1990, the entire town of Kaimū and part of the town of Kalapana were buried under 50 ft (15 m) of slow-moving lava from Kilauea. Despite the constant threat from the volcano, there are a few Kalapana residents who still choose to live alongside the lava.

Run! These scientists got a little too close when the eruption began in 1983.

**sun block** When Tambora, a volcano on the island of Sumbawa, Indonesia, erupted in 1815, the 200 million tons of sulfur dioxide gas that were ejected into the atmosphere reduced the amount of sunlight reaching the ground. This caused temperatures to drop dramatically all over the world, resulting in crop failures throughout Europe, and, in 1816, North America's "year without a summer," snow fell in June and New England experienced severe frosts in August.

**rapid growth** Just a week after it first appeared in a Mexican cornfield in 1943, the volcano Parícutin had reached a height of five stories, and a year later it stood 1,102 ft (336 m) tall.

**lava flow** Volcanic lava can reach a temperature of 2,300°F (1,250°C) and flow at speeds of up to 62 mph (100 km/h)—that's nearly three times as fast as an Olympic sprinter.

**constant eruption** Known as the "Lighthouse of the Mediterranean," 3,038-ft-high (926-m) Stromboli, off the coast of Italy, has been erupting almost continuously for over 20,000 years, emitting smoke and lava fragments about every 20 to 40 minutes.

**sole survivor** The city of St. Pierre (population 30,000) on the French-Caribbean island of Martinique was flattened in 1902 by the eruption of Mount Pelée, leaving just one survivor in the direct path of the volcano—Louis Auguste Cyparis. This man owed his life to the fact that he was being held in a poorly ventilated prison cell. After the disaster he was pardoned and joined the circus, until his death in 1929, as the "Prisoner of St. Pierre," earning a living by locking himself in an exact replica of his cell.

**deadly river** The 1783 Laki eruption in Iceland sent enough lava spewing from a 15-mi-long (25-km) crack to fill two deep river valleys and cover an area of more than 190 sq mi (500 sq km). The lava river, which was 100 ft (30 m) deep, engulfed villages and released poisonous gases that killed many of those who managed to escape its flow.

**nuclear noise** The 1883 eruption of Krakatoa, near Java, unleashed the power of 15,000 nuclear bombs with a noise so loud it could be heard nearly 3,100 mi (5,000 km) away. Before the eruption, the island of Krakatoa stood 1,476 ft (450 m) above sea level, but the blast leveled most of the island to 820 ft (250 m) below sea level.

As the lava builds in height, it tears road signs out of the ground before cooling to solid rock.

**undersea blast** There are at least 1,500 active volcanoes on the surface of the Earth and an estimated 10,000 volcanoes beneath the ocean. When an underwater volcano off the coast of Iceland erupted in 1963, it did so with such force that it punched through the sea and formed the 1-sq-mi (2.7-sq-km) Surtsey Island.

**volcano threat** Some 500 million people live close to active volcanoes—that's about one in 13 of the world's population. Popocatépetl, nicknamed El Popo, is just 33 mi (53 km) from Mexico City and every year it sends thousands of tons of gas and volcanic ash into the air.

Molten lava oozes toward the house.

The building finally succumbs to the heat.

## SPIDER CITY

A gigantic 600-ft-long (183-m) web appeared over the course of two weeks along the banks of a lake in a Texas state park. The unnerving sight at Lake Tawakoni drew more than 3,000 curious visitors on one weekend. Experts believe that the giant web was spun by thousands of spiders from several different species working together to trap as many insects as possible.

**R king carbone** Former flower grower Giorgio Carbone spent nearly 50 years championing the independence of the Italian village of Seborga, which he claimed should be recognized as a separate nation because it had never been formally included in the 19th-century unification of Italy. Proclaiming himself His Tremendousness Giorgio I, he ruled over 360 subjects until his death in 2009. He gave the principality its own currency, stamps, flag, and even a Latin motto—*Sub Umbra Sede* ("Sit in the Shade").

**R sewer fat** In a huge underground cleanup of central London in 2010, more than 1,000 tons of putrid fat were removed from sewers—enough fat to fill nine double-decker buses.

## DOWN THE DRAIN

This giant chasm in Lake Berryessa, California, is the biggest drain hole in the world, at 30 ft (9 m) in diameter. When the lake reaches capacity, water tips over the lip of the drain and surges down a 700-ft-long (213-m) concrete pipe to exit through the Monticello Dam some 300 ft (91 m) below. Swimming or even boating near the hole is strongly discouraged; in 1997, a swimmer strayed too close and was sucked into the powerful drain. Water gushes through the "glory hole," as locals have named it, at a rate of 362,057 gallons every second—that's enough to fill 15,000 bathtubs. When the lake's level is low, local skateboarders and BMX bikers ride the giant exit pipe.

**R inaccessible inn** Built in the middle of the 17th century, the Old Forge pub on the Knoydart peninsula in Northern Scotland can be reached only by boat or by walking 18 mi (29 km) from the nearest road over hills that rise to 3,500 ft (1,067 m).

**R moon lake** The 39,000-sq-mi (101,000-sq-km) lake on the north pole of Saturn's moon Titan is bigger than Lake Superior and most likely filled with liquid methane and ethane.

**R limestone forest** Water erosion has turned parts of Madagascar's Tsingy de Bemaraha National Park into forests of giant limestone spikes made of fossils and shellfish that died in the sea 200 million years ago.

**R acid drip** Snottites are colonies of bacteria that hang from the ceilings of caves and are similar to stalactites. The bacteria derive their energy from volcanic sulfur compounds and drip sulfuric acid that is as corrosive as battery acid.

**R dam cops** Nevada's Hoover Dam has its own police department whose duties include protecting the dam and safeguarding the lives of visitors and employees.

**haunted house** Josh Bond of Cuchillo, New Mexico, put his 130-year-old haunted house up for sale on the Internet auction site eBay. The listing offered 1,250 sq ft (115 sq m) of space spread over three bedrooms, an antique wood-burning stove, and the spirits of the restless dead.

**new ocean** A 2005 volcanic eruption caused a 35-mi-long (56-km) rift, 20 ft (6 m) wide in places, to open up in the Ethiopian desert in just days. In 2010, geologists predicted that the rift would slowly become a new ocean, as Africa begins to split in two.

**cursing festival** Every February, youngsters in the neighboring South Nepalese villages of Parsawa and Laxmipur hurl insults at each other and passersby in a ten-day cursing festival. On the final day of the festival, they set heaps of straw ablaze and celebrate the Hindu festival of Holi, which is marked by raucous "play" fights using powdered colored paints and water.

**more singapore** Thanks to numerous land reclamation projects, the island city-state of Singapore has 20 percent more land than it did four decades ago.

**cargo cult** For more than 60 years, villagers on the island of Tanna, Vanuatu, have worshiped "John Frum," an American they believe will one day return with a bounty of cargo. Clan leaders first saw the mysterious figure in the late 1930s and he is said to have appeared before them again during World War II, dressed in white like a Navy seaman. In his honor, the islanders celebrate John Frum Day every February 15.

**crystal clouds** Noctilucent clouds are formed by ice crystals 50 mi (80 km) above the Earth, on the very edge of space. They reflect sunlight at night, so that they glow.

**passion play** The village of Oberammergau, Bavaria, Germany, has held a Passion play, depicting the Crucifixion of Jesus, every ten years with few exceptions since 1633, when villagers swore an oath to perform the play every decade after their town was spared from the plague.

**tree dwellers** Members of the Korowai tribe of Papua New Guinea live in tree houses that are built as high as 150 ft (46 m) off the ground. They reach them by climbing vines or stairs carved into the trunks.

## Festival of the Skulls

Every year worshipers in the Bolivian city of La Paz offer gifts of flowers, food, and alcohol to the "snub noses"—decorated skulls of their relatives—to thank the dead for protecting the homes of the living. The "Day of the Skulls" festival is part of wider "Day of the Dead" rituals across Latin America, and traditionally entire skeletons were honored in this way.

## TAKING A LIBERTY

At 8.45 p.m. on the night of September 22, 2010, New York City photographer Jay Fine took this incredible photo of lightning striking the Statue of Liberty. He spent two hours braving the storm and took more than 80 shots before finally striking lucky. The iconic statue attracts over 600 bolts of lightning each year.

**last speaker** An ancient dialect called Bo, thought to date back 65,000 years, became extinct in 2010 after Boa Sr., the last person to speak it, died on a remote Indian island. At 85, Boa Sr. was the oldest member of the Great Andamanese Bo tribe before her death in Port Blair, the capital of Andaman and Nicobar Islands.

**dual rule** The U.S. city of Bristol straddles the borders of Virginia and Tennessee and has two governments, one for each half.

**burning river** The Cuyahoga River in Ohio was so polluted in the 20th century that it caught fire more than half a dozen times.

**volcano video** In May 2009, U.S. scientists videotaped an undersea volcanic eruption off the coast of Samoa, 4,000 ft (1,220 m) beneath the surface—the first time a sea floor eruption had been filmed.

**rabbit island** It cost more than one million dollars to rid the tiny Scottish island of Canna of rats in 2006, and now, less than four years later, it has been overrun with thousands of rabbits—because there are no rats to keep their numbers down! The island's only restaurant has responded by adding a number of rabbit dishes to its menu.

**mail boat** Since 1916, a boat has been delivering mail to dozens of homes on Lake Geneva, Wisconsin—and because it never stops, teenage carriers are hired to jump off the moving boat, put the mail in mailboxes on the dock, then scurry back on board, hopefully without falling into the lake.

**huge hailstone** A giant hailstone that fell in Vivian, South Dakota, on the night of July 23, 2010, measured 8 in (20 cm) in diameter, 18½ in (47 cm) in circumference, and weighed 1 lb 15 oz (900 g)! This and other ice missiles were so large that some punched holes into roofs big enough for householders to put their arm through, while other hailstones gouged holes in the ground more than an inch deep.

**watery grave** As drought conditions dried up a pond in Aligarh, Uttar Pradesh, India, in May 2009, 98 human skulls were found at the bottom.

**sparsely populated** The state of Nevada covers an area about the size of Britain and Ireland combined, but has only 70 towns, whereas the British Isles has more than 40,000.

**shifting city** The Chilean earthquake of February 27, 2010, moved the city of Concepción about 10 ft (3 m) to the west. The quake was so powerful that it shortened the length of the day by 1.26 microseconds, and even Buenos Aires—840 mi (1,350 km) from Concepción—shifted by 1.5 in (3.8 cm).

## Pink Lake

Lake Retba (the Rose Lake), situated 25 mi (40 km) north of Dakar in Senegal, has pink water, which can even turn purple in strong sunshine. The 1-sq-mi (3-sq-km) lake gets its unusual color from unique cyan bacteria in the water and also from its very high salt content.

**buried lake** At 155 mi (250 km) long and 31 mi (50 km) wide, Lake Vostok is about the same size as Lake Ontario—but lies beneath 2.5 mi (4 km) of Antarctic ice.

**ginkgo stink** The ginkgo tree species, native to Asia, is so resilient that several survived the atomic bomb blast in Hiroshima, Japan—but its smell is proving its downfall in Iowa City, United States. When the tree drops its seed shells, it produces a sticky mess that smells of rotten eggs, creating a sanitation problem for the city.

**floating stump** The Old Man of the Lake, a 30-ft-tall (9-m) tree stump, has floated around Crater Lake, Oregon, for more than 100 years. During that time, high winds and waves have caused it to move great distances—in one three-month period of observation in 1938 it traveled more than 62 mi (100 km).

**hot water** At the bottom of shallow bodies of very salty water, temperatures can reach 176°F (80°C) and stay that way 24 hours a day.

**river logjam** Over several centuries, a natural logjam in North America's Red River grew to a length of more than 160 mi (256 km). When people began clearing it in the early 1800s, it took 40 years to complete the task.

**lightning storm** In just one hour on September 9, 2010, Hong Kong was hit by 13,102 lightning strikes. The violent electrical storm contained wind gusts of 62 mph (100 km/h) and caused power cuts that left people trapped in elevators.

**widespread snow** On February 12, 2010, all of the states in the United States except Hawaii received some snow.

**fog nets** Communities in Chile's Atacama Desert use nets to catch the morning fog—the only accessible fresh water in the region. One of the driest places on Earth, it only gets significant rainfall two to four times a century, and in some parts of the desert no rain has ever been recorded.

**asteroid blast** A 33-ft-wide (10-m) asteroid exploded with the energy of three Hiroshima atom bombs in the atmosphere above Indonesia on October 8, 2009. The asteroid hit the atmosphere at about 45,000 mph (72,000 km/h), causing a blast that was estimated by NASA to be equivalent to 55,000 tons of TNT, and which was heard by monitoring stations 10,000 mi (16,000 km) away. There was no damage on the ground, however, because it occurred at least 9.3 mi (15 km) above the Earth's surface.

**life on mars?** Huge plumes of methane—a gas that can indicate the presence of living organisms—have been found on the northern side of Mars. The methane may come from live organisms or from the decomposing remains of dead ones.

## RIPLEY RESEARCH

In winter, starlings flock in groups of anything from a few thousand to 20 million birds—huge numbers that turn the sky black. Flying at speeds of more than 20 mph (32 km/h) while they search for somewhere safe to roost for the night, they group together to avoid predators such as sparrowhawks and peregrine falcons. In flight, each starling is able to track seven other birds—irrespective of distance—and this is what enables them to maintain such a cohesive overall shape.

## STARLING FLOCK

Thousands of starlings in the sky above Taunton in Somerset, England, formed the shape of one giant starling! These acrobatic birds have created many different patterns in the sky, including a rabbit, a rubber duck, and a turtle.

# Ripley's Believe It or Not! crazy world

**leaning skyscraper** The 530-ft-high (160-m) Capital Gate building in Abu Dhabi leans at an angle of 18 degrees—four times more than Italy's famous Leaning Tower of Pisa. The new 35-story building achieves this angle by using staggered floor plates from the 12th floor up.

**towering tent** A giant tent 490 ft (150 m) high opened in Astana, Kazakhstan, in 2010. Designed to withstand the nation's extreme variations in temperature, the Khan Shatyr Entertainment Center took four years to build. Made from three layers of transparent plastic, it stands on a 650-ft (200-m) concrete base and houses shops, restaurants, movie theaters, and even an artificial beach and running track.

**security cage** After being burgled eight times in six months, 80-year-old Chinese grandmother Ling Wan turned her apartment in Changsha into a giant birdcage. She sealed up the stairs and built an iron cage around the apartment so that the only way in and out is via a ladder that is securely locked on her balcony.

**capsule hotels** Japan's capsule hotels have rooms that measure roughly 7 x 4 x 3 ft (2.1 x 1.2 x 0.9 m)— not much bigger than a coffin! They are stacked side by side on two levels, with steps providing access to the upper capsule. Some hotels have more than 700 capsules.

**light tower** The Eiffel Tower in Paris, France, weighs less than a cylinder of air occupying the same dimensions. The force of the wind causes the top of the lightweight metal tower to sway up to 3 in (7.6 cm).

**sole occupant** Owing to the recession, for three years Les Harrington was the only resident of a 2.4-acre (1-ha) luxury village in Essex, England, that boasted 58 cottages and apartments.

**007 tribute** For a 2009 New Year's Eve party, James Bond fanatics Simon and Angie Mullane spent four months and $4,500 transforming their Dorset, England, home into a 007 movie set. Guests were greeted at a homemade checkpoint manned by dummies dressed in authentic East German border guard uniforms bought on the Internet, while a Sean Connery mannequin dangled from a real hang glider in the garden.

**luxury igloo** In January 2010, Jimmy Grey built a luxury, four-room igloo in the yard of his home in Aquilla, Ohio. The igloo had 6-ft-high (1.8-m) ceilings and an entertainment room, complete with cable TV (plugged into an outlet in his garage) and surround-sound stereo.

## Container Store

Shoppers visiting the flagship Freitag bag store in Zurich, Switzerland, certainly need a head for heights, as the building is made from a dizzying stack of used steel shipping containers. It consists of 17 containers of which nine form the 85-ft-high (26-m) tower. The recycling theme of the building mirrors the bags sold inside, which are made from such items as old truck tarpaulins, bicycle inner tubes, and car seat belts.

## TUNNEL VISION

Over a period of four weeks, sculptors Dan Havel and Dean Ruck from Houston, Texas, transformed two connected properties to create a large, tunnel-like vortex, making it look as if the interior of the buildings had exploded. The outer skin of the two houses—made from planks of pine—was peeled off and used to create a 60-ft-long (18-m) spiral, which narrowed to a width of about 2 ft (60 cm) at the far end.

**poop light** In 2010, a park in Cambridge, Massachusetts, had a street light that was powered by dog poop. Created by artist Matthew Mazzotta, the "Park Spark" project encouraged dog walkers to collect their pets' poop in biodegradable bags and drop it into one of two 500-gal (1,900-l) steel tanks. Microbes in the waste gave off methane gas, which was fed through a second tank to the lamp and burned off.

**mecca clock** The Royal Mecca Clock, located on a skyscraper in Mecca, Saudi Arabia, has four amazing faces each measuring 151 ft (46 m) in diameter—that's more than six times larger than the faces of London's Big Ben clock. Over 90 million pieces of colored glass mosaic decorate the sides of the clock, which is visible from every part of the city. On special occasions, 16 bands of vertical lights shoot from the clock 6 mi (10 km) into the sky.

**lost language** The writing on the back of a letter discovered in 2008 by archeologists at a 17th-century dig site reveals a previously unknown language spoken by indigenous peoples in northern Peru. The letter, found under a pile of clay bricks in a collapsed church near Trujillo, shows a column of numbers written in Spanish and translated into a mysterious language that has been extinct for at least 400 years.

**home wrecker** In February 2010, a man bulldozed his $350,000 Moscow, Ohio, home when a bank claimed it as collateral for outstanding debt.

**whistle blowers** Officials in Alor Setar, Malaysia, blow whistles loudly at litterbugs in the hope of shaming them into never littering again.

**rotating house** A rotating house north of Sydney, Australia, guarantees Luke Everingham and his family a different view every time they wake up. The octagonal-shaped house sits on a turntable powered by a small electric motor and controlled by a computer, which allows it to move on demand, completing a full rotation in half an hour.

**vast collection** The British Museum in London has 80,000 objects on display—but that is only one per cent of its total collection.

**railroad room** The Washington Hotel in Tokyo, Japan, has created a special room for model railway enthusiasts to sleep in. It includes a grand model of the local area, complete with working railroads. Train lovers can bring their own models or, alternatively, the hotel will happily provide some.

**school mascot** The mascot of Yuma Union High School in Yuma, Arizona, is a criminal dressed in a prison uniform. It was adopted nearly a century ago after classes were held in a prison building when the original school burned down.

## CIGARETTTE HOUSE

A house in Hangzhou, Zhejiang Province, China, is brightly decorated throughout with more than 30,000 empty cigarette packets. The occupant collected them over a period of six years and has even created seats and tables from the empty packs.

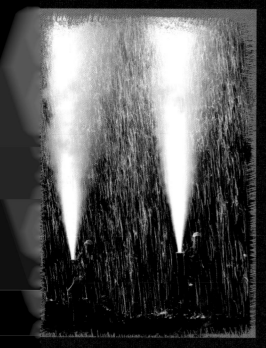

## FLAMING FESTIVAL

Each year the city of Toyohashi in Japan hosts an extreme fire festival. Fearless volunteers launch enormous homemade bamboo fireworks, known as *tezutsu hanabi*, which explode inches from their face. The 300-year-old festival sets off 12,000 fireworks and can draw more than 350 homemade cannons that spew fire up to 65 ft (20 m) into the sky.

**luminous beams** A mysterious "rain" of vertical luminous beams appeared for nearly an hour in the night sky above Xiamen, China, in July 2010. At first there were just five beams, hanging low in the sky, but soon the number increased to 50. A local observatory confirmed that it was definitely not a meteor shower.

**glass elephant** Built on top of an old coalminer's washroom, the Glass Elephant in the Maximillianpark, Hamm, Germany—designed in 1984 by artist and architect Horst Rellecke—stands an amazing 115 ft (35 m) tall.

**mud volcano** A mud volcano in Sidoarjo, East Java, Indonesia, spews enough scalding mud daily to fill 50 Olympic-size swimming pools. Since its first eruption in 2006, it has buried 12 villages.

**royal shrine** Mehrangarh Fort in Jodhpur, Rajasthan, India, has a shrine bearing carvings of the handprints of royal widows that committed *suttee*—a ceremony in which women were burned alive upon the funeral pyre of their husbands.

**falling ice** In 2008, a 6-lb (2.7-kg) chunk of ice fell from the sky, crashed through the roof of a home in York Township, Pennsylvania, and hit Mary Ann Foster, who was sleeping, on the head. It turned out to be atmospheric ice, formed when moisture in the atmosphere freezes into small ice balls, which then bump into each other and sometimes attach themselves together to create larger chunks.

**underground home** Unable to afford a bigger house, retired Chinese miner Chen Xinnian tunneled out a one-bedroom apartment measuring 540-sq-ft (50-sq-m) beneath his existing home in Zhengzhou, Henan Province. The apartment is 20 ft (6 m) underground and is so cool that food does not need to be kept in a refrigerator.

**hard wood** Ironwood trees—including the black ironwood species that is native to the United States—have wood so dense that it won't float in water. It sinks instead.

**river ritual** More than ten million devotees from across the country came to Haridwar, India, in February 2010 for the Kumbh Mela Festival, held here once every 12 years, to bathe in the River Ganges.

**desert snow** China's largest desert, the Taklamakan, covers approximately 125,000 sq mi (325,000 sq km) and, in January 2008, snow blanketed the entire area for the first time ever.

**violent quake** On February 7, 1812, a massive earthquake struck near New Madrid, Missouri, and shook so violently that the Mississippi River flowed backward for several hours.

**lunar pit** Photographs of the Moon taken from the Japanese Kaguya spacecraft revealed a giant pit about 427 ft (130 m) in diameter on the lunar surface—that's large enough to swallow an entire football field.

**hanging coffins** The Bo people, an ethnic group from China's Sichuan Province that disappeared hundreds of years ago, hung the coffins of their dead on the sides of cliffs. The coffins were lowered on ropes from above to rest on precipices or wooden stakes. Some were hung as high as 425 ft (130 m) above ground, as the belief was that the higher the coffin was placed, the more propitious it was for the dead. The earliest hanging coffins found in the region date back 2,500 years.

## CRACKERS

During the Chinese Lantern Festival celebrations in Taiwan, it's customary for onlookers to launch firecrackers at a shirtless man who represents the god of wealth. The more fireworks that hit their intended target, the more successful the firework thrower will become. This dangerous-looking ritual has been performed in the area for over 50 years.

## Fire in the Hole

In the middle of a remote desert in Turkmenistan, the Darvaza crater is continually ablaze. The 200-ft-wide (60-m) chasm was created when a sinkhole collapsed under a gas-mining rig in 1971. The miners started a fire to burn off the gas, but it just kept coming and the crater has been burning ever since. If you can stand the heat, it is possible to walk right to the edge of the hole, which is 65 ft (20 m) deep.

# • FAIR FACTS •

- The electric lighting for the 1934 Fair came from 250,000 incandescent bulbs and totaled 30,000,000,000 candlepower—enough electricity to supply the needs of a town of 10,000 people.

- More than six million people rode in the Sky Ride elevators in the first 5½ months of the Fair.

- If all the steel cable in the Sky Ride had been stretched out in a single cable, it would have been more than 100 mi (160 km) long.

- The fountain at the 1934 Fair shot water 45 ft (14 m) into the air, pouring out 68,000 gal (260,000 l) a minute.

- A restaurant seating 3,500 people was a replica of the Old Heidelberg Inn, Germany.

- On October 26, 1933, the 776-ft-long (238-m) German airship *Graf Zeppelin* visited the Fair.

- The 1933 Fair employed 350 painters to create a "carnival of color" by using 25 different exterior colors and 36 interior colors of more than 25,000 gal (113,500 l) of paint to cover 10,500,000 sq ft (975,500 sq m) of surface area.

## All the fun of the Fair

*The Fair featured a multitude of dazzling exhibitions and displays that wowed audiences both by presenting cutting-edge technologies and by celebrating the diverse nature of the world in which they lived. Alongside exhibits demonstrating homes and cars of the future were re-creations of villages from over a dozen different countries—including England, France, Italy, Morocco, Belgium, and Mexico—and newborn babies in incubators, which were a great scientific novelty at the time. Also on show was the ship belonging to Antarctic explorer Richard Byrd, and "Midget City," which was full of miniature houses inhabited by 60 "Lilliputians"—small people who included 18-year-old, 18.75-in-tall (46.8-cm) Margaret Ann Robinson, who weighed only 19 lb (8.6 kg).*

**star light** The Fair was opened in spectacular style—when its lights were switched on with energy gathered from the rays of a distant star, Arcturus. With the aid of powerful telescopes, Arcturus' rays were focused on light-absorbent photoelectric cells in a number of astronomical observatories and then transformed into electrical energy, which was transmitted to Chicago. Arcturus was chosen because it was thought to be 40 light years away from Earth, and Chicago's previous World Fair had been 40 years earlier in 1893.

**assembly line** The central feature of the Fair's General Motors building was a complete automobile assembly plant, where 1,000 people at a time could watch cars being made from start to finish.

**rainbow lights** At night, the city and Lake Michigan were illuminated by an ever-changing rainbow provided by a color scintillator composed of 3-ft-wide (1-m) arc searchlights arranged in two banks of 12. The scintillator operators changed the color filters and the positions of the searchlight beams according to a prearranged schedule.

**steel house** Among the innovative exhibits at the Homes of Tomorrow Exposition was a fireproof house built from steel and baked iron enamel. After the Fair it was moved to Palos Heights, Illinois, where it remained until being demolished in 1992.

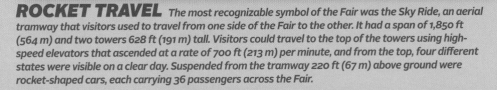

SKY RIDE, CHICAGO WORLD'S FAIR
36A29
3A-H8

HAVOLINE THERMOMETER *Century of Progress International Exposition* CHICAGO 1933

## ROCKET TRAVEL
*The most recognizable symbol of the Fair was the Sky Ride, an aerial tramway that visitors used to travel from one side of the Fair to the other. It had a span of 1,850 ft (564 m) and two towers 628 ft (191 m) tall. Visitors could travel to the top of the towers using high-speed elevators that ascended at a rate of 700 ft (213 m) per minute, and from the top, four different states were visible on a clear day. Suspended from the tramway 220 ft (67 m) above ground were rocket-shaped cars, each carrying 36 passengers across the Fair.*

## HIGH-RISE TEMPERATURE
*Another principal landmark of the Fair was the 218-ft-high (67-m), 21-story thermometer that was sponsored by the motor oil manufacturer Havoline. The air temperature was shown by means of neon light tubes on the outside of the building.*

▶

# Chicago World's Fair

Between 1933 and 1934, about 48 million people visited the Chicago World's Fair—a showcase of thousands of exhibits including the latest scientific, architectural, and transport innovations.

The Century of Progress Exposition, as the Fair was known, was held to commemorate Chicago's 100th anniversary and to illustrate the amazing technological developments that had taken place worldwide in that time. It was staged on an area of 427 acres (173 ha) along the shoreline of Lake Michigan, and opened on May 27, 1933. It closed on November 12, but had proved so popular that it was re-opened the following May, and ran until the end of October 1934.

Also appearing at the Fair was the first-ever Ripley's Odditorium, which was one of the most popular crowd-pullers, attracting over two million visitors. Show-business agent Clint Finney had been assigned by Robert Ripley to find the best performers to appear at this Odditorium, and Finney managed the show in 1933 and 1934 with C.C. Pyle. With their help, Ripley scoured the world for unusual performers, his "human rarities and oddities." Ripley's many international contacts also sent him photographs and telegrams suggesting possible people to include.

A CENTURY OF PROGRESS
CHICAGO 1933
INTERNATIONAL EXPOSITION

SERIAL No. 11303    1933

IDENTIFICATION CARD
(NOT A PASS)

S. B. Ricketts         2
EMPLOYEE OF CONCESSIONAIRE
International Oddities, Inc.
AT A CENTURY OF PROGRESS

PAY ROLL No.

S.B. Ricketts
EMPLOYEE'S SIGNATURE
ACCEPTED SUBJECT TO CONDITIONS ON PASS
ISSUED BY
A CENTURY OF PROGRESS
Lenox R. Lohr
General Manager
FORM S.C.44

NOTICE TO KULI ALI BEI, FAKIR CEKANAVICIUS AND OTHERS

People with peculiar characteristics or peculiar physical built (freaks), are wanted for worlds fair in Chicago, from June 1 to November 1, 1934. A certain firm will pay a round trip passage fare and living expenses such as meals, board etc. to all such exponents that will be demonstrated at the fair. The firm will cover all expenses and pay wages to guides who will accompany non English speaking exponents. It will also furnish all documentary ... ities for the entrance into the United

Postal Telegraph
THE INTERNATIONAL SYSTEM

Commercial Cables    All America Cables
Mackay    Radio

New York    Aug. 21, 1933

... ain Goic
Imperial Hotel
Dubrovnik    Jugu Slavia

... ge to bring small man and father to America at once ... ay all expenses and reasonable salaries    Send their ... immediately

Ripley

Official Post Card of
RIPLEY'S
"BELIEVE-IT-OR-NOT" ODDITORIUM
A CENTURY OF PROGRESS

The name & address on this card was written upside down and backwards and at ease. Now see if you can read this just fill in the closed spaces, not the open ones.
WHATS 1/2 of 12, vy
J. D. MORENO & CO., PRINTERS, CHICAGO, U.S.A.
CUT IN HALF

POST CARD
CENTURY OF PROGRESS
CHICAGO 1933

Robert L. Ripley
c/o New York American,
South Street,
New York City,
N.Y.

Postal Telegraph
THE INTERNATIONAL SYSTEM

Commercial Cables    All America Cables
Mackay    Radio

This is a full rate Telegram, Cablegram or Radiogram unless otherwise indicated by signal in the check or in the address.
DL    DAY LETTER
NM    NIGHT MESSAGE
NL    NIGHT LETTER
LCO    DEFERRED CABLE
NLT    NIGHT CABLE LETTER
WLT    WEEK END CABLE LETTER
RADIOGRAM

...119 54 WIRELESS COLLECT VIA MACKAYRADIO=N MANILA 1048A MAR 7 1934

...T RIPLEY KINGSYN=

...:NEWYORKNY (RIPLEY KINGS FEATURES SYNDICATE 235 EAST 45 ST)=

...BTAINABLE TWELVE MALE FEMALE PRIEST MAGNUNUS FIRE WALKERS
...LAST DAGGER CEREMONY PRECEDING WALK STOP OBTAINABLE UP
... PONTOC IGOROT HEADHUNTERS ARMS WAR

Believe It or Not
ODDITORIUM

INTERNATIONAL ODDITIES, INCORPORAT
666 LAKE SHORE DRIVE
CHICAGO, ILLINOIS

May 8, 1934.

"BELIEVE-IT-OR-NOT" EXHIBITION
CENTURY OF PROGRESS
1 TO OCTOBER 31, 1934.

Memo for Mr. Simpson:

In regard to the Chinese man t
you believe could be dressed in Korean religious co
and be a good attraction, beg to advise that there
many giant                    feet tall wh
tower ove
any goo

A CENTURY OF PROGRESS—1933
, ILLINOIS

Billy Cunningham
817 So. 4th St
Louisville Ky.

Ripley Ripley

Believe It or Not Believe It or Not

W. A. Cunningham
817 So. 4th St
Louisville
N.Y.

HAITI.    OBTAIN "PINK MAN" FR
          THIS IS GOOD,    DO
STORY ABOUT PILL.

CAN'T GET BORNEO BELLES
    "    "  CARVED FACE MEN
BUT TRY ALEKO E. LILLIS
P.O. BOX 3220 Manila.    Cable addres
                                AEOLUS

OBTAIN William D'Andrea
88 SOUTH C

## At Chicago Exhibit of Believe-It-Or-Nots

Thousands of Americans who have followed the famous
Believe-It-Or-Not Cartoons of Robert Ripley are seeing
the actual Believe-It-Or-Nots housed in the palatial Ripley "Odditorium" at the Chicago Century of Progress. Included
among the exhibits are (left) Singhlee, a Hindu who can grasp a
red-hot metal bar and put it to his mouth; (below left) Albert Nelson
and his one-man mechanical band of thirty instruments; and (below
right) Blystone, the rice writer.

F L BLYSTONE
of ARDARA, Pa
WROTE 2871 LEGIBLE LETTERS

Head contortionist ▶ Martin Laurello discovered his unusual ability as a child and spent many years mastering his stunt of looking backward while walking forward, baffling scientists and amazing Odditorium audiences.

◀ Grace McDaniels complained about her early billing as "the ugliest woman in the world," but nevertheless was a popular sideshow draw for many years, later becoming known by her preferred moniker, "The Mule-Faced Woman." After fielding several marriage proposals, she settled down and had a son, Elmer (pictured here), who later became her manager.

▲ Freda Pushnik from Pennsylvania was born with no arms or legs, but she was determined to master everyday tasks. Aged just ten years old, she wowed audiences at the 1933 World's Fair with her cheerful repartee and demonstrations of writing and sewing. Freda performed in Ripley's Odditoriums for six years, and went on to have a successful sideshow career before retiring from the stage in the 1950s.

ELECTRICAL GROUP

ENCHANTED ISLAND

HORTICULTURAL BLDG.

PABST BLUE RIBBON CASINO
HOLLYWOOD CLUB

HALL OF RELIGION

BYRD'S ANARCTIC SHIP

Habu Koller ▶ from Germany could lift over 100 lb (45 kg) using a hole in his tongue. According to his Ripley backstory, Habu reportedly received a split tongue as punishment in Asia after refusing to bear arms in World War I.

Professor A. L. Morrell, the "Jack-Knife King," was billed as the world's greatest whittler. Assisted by his wife, he wowed audiences with his astonishing exhibit of carved objects displayed in a variety of small-necked bottles. ▼

Charles Romano, ▶ the "Rubber Arm Man," could twist and turn and throw his arms around in such a way that audiences were amazed that he could return his body to its normal shape and position.

More than two million visitors flocked to the Ripley's Odditorium to see sword-swallowers, fire-eaters, eye-poppers, and many other curiosities. The attraction proved so popular that Ripley's founder, Robert Ripley, went on to open many other Odditoriums across the United States.

*dditorium*

STREETS OF PARIS
23RD ST. ENTRANCE
A. & P. CARNIVAL
BELGIAN VILLAGE
PANTHEON
ORIENTAL VILLAGE
THE MIDWAY
GETTYS
PAN
A CENTURY OF PR
CH

OF. A.L. MORRELL
JACK KNIFE KING:

Egyptian Hadji Ali could ▶ drink up to 50 glasses of water in quick succession and then return it all to a receptacle in a steady stream, turning himself into a "human fountain." He also swallowed a range of other items before regurgitating them in any order requested.

# Ripley's Believe It or Not!

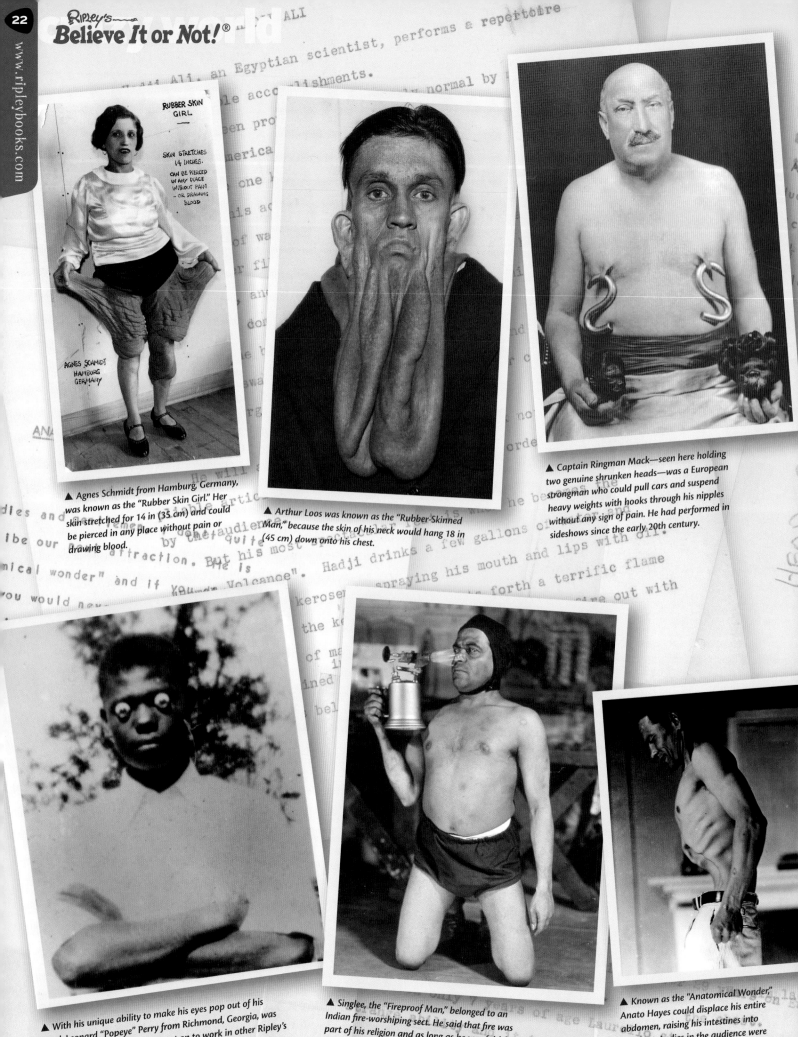

▲ Agnes Schmidt from Hamburg, Germany, was known as the "Rubber Skin Girl." Her skin stretched for 14 in (35 cm) and could be pierced in any place without pain or drawing blood.

RUBBER SKIN GIRL

SKIN STRETCHES 14 INCHES.

CAN BE PIERCED IN ANY PLACE WITHOUT PAIN – OR DRAWING BLOOD

AGNES SCHMIDT HAMBURG GERMANY

▲ Arthur Loos was known as the "Rubber-Skinned Man," because the skin of his neck would hang 18 in (45 cm) down onto his chest.

▲ Captain Ringman Mack—seen here holding two genuine shrunken heads—was a European strongman who could pull cars and suspend heavy weights with hooks through his nipples without any sign of pain. He had performed in sideshows since the early 20th century.

▲ With his unique ability to make his eyes pop out of his head, Leonard "Popeye" Perry from Richmond, Georgia, was an Odditorium sensation. He went on to work in other Ripley's Odditoriums for many years after the Chicago Fair.

▲ Singlee, the "Fireproof Man," belonged to an Indian fire-worshiping sect. He said that fire was part of his religion and as long as he was faithful to his fire god, fire could not harm him.

▲ Known as the "Anatomical Wonder," Anato Hayes could displace his entire abdomen, raising his intestines into his chest. Ladies in the audience were advised to "get a good firm grip on [their] escort's arm" before he appeared!

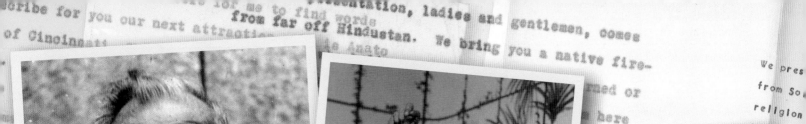

▲ J.T. Saylors from Georgia had never demonstrated his talent for jaw-dislocation and pulling funny faces professionally, despite offers from show people and motion picture companies, until he appeared at the Odditorium in Chicago.

▲ Kanichka, or "The Man with the Ostrich Stomach," swallowed billiard balls, goldfish, silver dollars, wristwatches, and doorknobs—and would then regurgitate them. As a finale, he would swallow electric lights, visible within his stomach when switched on. He was described as having an ostrich stomach because they swallow stones.

▲ Lydia McPherson of Los Angeles was billed as having the longest red hair in the world, which stretched 7 ft 5 in (2.3 m) in length.

▲ Sword-swallower Joseph Grendol had worked a season for the Ringling Circus before joining Ripley's Odditorium. He would swallow a 20-in (50-cm) bayonet attached to the butt of a rifle and then fire the gun while the bayonet was in his stomach!

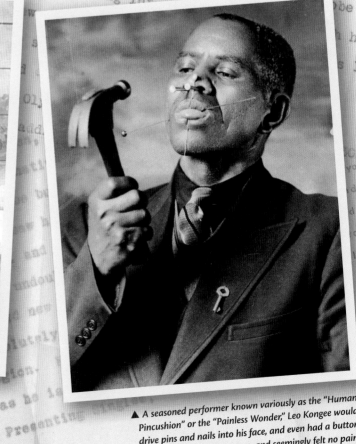

▲ A seasoned performer known variously as the "Human Pincushion" or the "Painless Wonder," Leo Kongee would drive pins and nails into his face, and even had a button sewn onto his tongue, and seemingly felt no pain.

# Ripley's Believe It or Not!® crazy world

## RIVER RUNS RED

The water rushing over Cameron Falls, Alberta, Canada, turned pinky red following a heavy storm. The phenomenon was caused by high levels of rain that washed a red sediment called argolite from 1,500-million-year-old rocks into the river.

**underwater meeting** In October 2009, the government of the low-lying islands of the Maldives in the Indian Ocean held an underwater meeting to highlight the dangers of global warming. Dressed in full scuba gear, President Nasheed and ten colleagues took part in the 30-minute meeting at a depth of 20 ft (6 m) off the coast, near the country's capital Malé. Most of the Maldives is barely 3 ft (1 m) above sea level, and scientists fear it could be uninhabitable in fewer than 100 years.

**time tunnel** Ramchandra Das of Bihar, India, spent 14 years cutting a tunnel 33 ft (10 m) long and 13 ft (4 m) wide through a mountain with only a hammer and chisel so that his neighbors could avoid an arduous 4½-mi (7-km) trek around the mountain to work and so that he could park his truck closer to home.

**hidden home** Sharon Simpson created a luxurious tent home—complete with solar shower and satellite TV—on a busy traffic circle in the center of Derby, England. She lived there unnoticed for five months and moved out only when leaves falling off nearby bushes took away her privacy.

**souvenir snowball** For more than 30 years, Prena Thomas of Lakeland, Florida, has kept a snowball in her freezer—the souvenir of a rare Florida snowfall. When 2 in (5 cm) of snow fell on the normally balmy state on January 19, 1977, she was so surprised that she collected some of the snow and put it in her freezer.

**piping hot** The sidewalks of Klamath Falls, Oregon, are kept free from snow and ice—and therefore safe for pedestrians—by hot-water pipes that run underneath them.

**new castle** Since 1997, some 50 workers in central France have been building a new medieval castle using only the tools and materials that were available in the 13th century. The brainchild of local landowner Michel Guyot, the Château de Guédelon is being built from sandstone, and when it's finished in around 2022 will boast a main tower more than 90 ft (27 m) tall.

## BROCKEN SPECTER

Local climbers in the Polish Tatra Mountains believe that if they witness a Brocken Specter—their own giant shadow projected on thick cloud below them—then they are doomed to die on the mountain. The phenomenon is named after the Brocken Mountain in Germany.

**jet power** The Dubai Fountain, located beside the Burj Khalifa skyscraper in Dubai, is almost 900 ft (275 m) long and can fire jets of water 500 ft (150 m) into the air.

**ice man** Nicknamed the "Ice man of Ladakh," retired Indian engineer Chewang Norphel has tackled environmental problems by building more than a dozen new glaciers in the Himalayas. He constructs his own glaciers by diverting meltwater through pipes into artificial lakes. Shaded by the mountains and kept in place by dams, the water in the lakes remains frozen until springtime when it melts and feeds the rivers below, which in turn irrigate surrounding farmland. He decided to act after melting glaciers caused floods that destroyed homes and crops.

**time travel** Russia has no fewer than nine different time zones—and the eastern region of Chukotka (just across the Bering Strait from Alaska) is nine hours ahead of Kaliningrad in the extreme west of the country. There were 11 time zones in Russia until two were scrapped in 2010.

**storm hole** A Guatemala City clothing factory and an entire traffic intersection were swallowed by a cavernous sinkhole, which suddenly opened up during a tropical storm in 2010. The sinkhole was almost perfectly round and measured 65 ft (20 m) wide and 100 ft (30 m) deep.

**purple snow** In March 2010, purple snow fell in Stavropol, southern Russia. The unusual coloration was the result of dust from Africa rising in a massive cyclone to layers of the upper atmosphere and then mixing with regular snow clouds over Russia.

# Freeze that Fire!

When water was used to put out a burning building in Montreal, Quebec, Canada, in the late 19th century, the air temperature was so cold that the water quickly turned to ice.

St. James Street Fire, Montreal.

*Ripley's*
# Believe It or Not!

## CRAZY KINK

A 7.1-magnitude earthquake near Canterbury, New Zealand, in September 2010 caused rail tracks in the region to buckle alarmingly. A train engineer managed to stop his two engines just 100 ft (30 m) short of this crazy kink. Repairs involved removing the crippled rails and replacing them with new rails that measured about 6½ ft (2 m) shorter than the originals.

**ring of fire** Three-quarters of the world's active and dormant volcanoes exist within the 25,000-mi (40,000-km) Ring of Fire, situated along the edges of the Pacific Ocean. Among them is Alaska's Mount Redoubt, which erupted in March 2009, sending a plume of smoke nearly 10 mi (16 km) into the air.

**shooting spores** *Pilobolis* fungi live in animal dung and are less than 0.4 in (1 cm) tall, but they shoot packets of spores up to 6 ft (1.8 m) in the air to reproduce.

**meteorite crater** Max Rocca, an amateur geologist from Buenos Aires, Argentina, found an ancient meteorite crater 31 mi (50 km) across in the Colombian rainforest—by examining satellite pictures. His interest was aroused after he detected a near-perfect semicircular curve in the Vichada River.

**young star** On November 7, 2008, 14-year-old amateur astronomer Caroline Moore of Warwick, New York, discovered a supernova—and the exploding star she found (dubbed SN 2008ha) was about 1,000 times dimmer than a typical supernova.

**multiple eclipse** Solar eclipses are a major phenomenon here on Earth, but the planet Jupiter, because it has 50 confirmed moons, can have multiple eclipses happening simultaneously.

**nuclear reactions** The Sun's core has enough hydrogen to continue fueling its nuclear reactions for another five billion years.

**new cloud** Meteorologists believe they have discovered a new type of cloud. The Cloud Appreciation Society has named it *asperatus*, after the Latin word for "rough," on account of its rough and choppy underside. If it becomes officially recognized, it will be the first new cloud type since 1951.

**black hole** NASA has found a gigantic black hole 100 million times the mass of the Sun, feeding off gas, dust, and stars at the center of a galaxy, 50 million light-years away.

**toxic lake** Argentina's Lake Diamante is filled with thriving bacteria despite being oxygen depleted, hyper-saline, spectacularly toxic, and bombarded with ultraviolet radiation.

**school climb** Erping Village Elementary School in Sichuan Province, China, is built on a platform nearly 10,000 ft (3,050 m) up a remote mountainside. Until 2010, when a new steel stairway was built on the cliff, students could get to school only by climbing a series of rickety, homemade wooden ladders. The school's two teachers had to escort the children up and down the ladders because the journey was so dangerous and exhausting.

## DRY RUN

The U.S. side of the mighty Niagara Falls was nearly as dry as a desert for five months in 1969. Engineers stopped the waterfall for the first time in 12,000 years by building a temporary 600-ft-wide (180-m) dam from 27,800 tons of rock and diverting the flow of the Niagara River over the larger Horseshoe Falls on the Canadian side. The work was carried out to remove a large quantity of loose rock from the base of the U.S. side of the Falls, which, if left in place, might eventually prevent the waterfall from flowing at all. To delay the gradual erosion of the U.S. side, faults were also mechanically strengthened. When the task was finished and the dam was blown up, 60,000 gal (227,000 l) of water once again thundered over the U.S. side of the Falls every second.

## Ice House

The Cleveland Harbor West Pierhead Lighthouse on the shores of Lake Erie, Ohio, looked more like a fairy-tale castle in December 2010 when it became completely covered in layers of ice. High winds caused waves to crash over the lighthouse, where the water then froze in the bitterly cold temperatures.

**phone access** Only about one-third of India's population has access to modern sanitation—but nearly half of the population has a cell phone!

**narrow house** A three-story house in Brighton, East Sussex, England, is just 6 ft (1.8 m) wide. Owners Iain and Rachel Boyle bought the former donkey-cart shed for just $12,000 in 1998, but have turned it into such a stylish home—complete with a mezzanine bedroom—that they now rent it out.

**one-way traffic** Between 2004 and 2009, nearly 10,000 North Koreans defected to South Korea—while only two people went in the other direction!

**hot ash** Volcanic avalanches of hot ash, rock fragments, and gas—known as pyroclastic flows—can move at 150 mph (240 km/h) and are capable of knocking down and burning everything in their path.

**judge numbers** India has 11 judges for every million people, while the United States has 110 per million—ten times as many.

**reduced alphabet** Rotokas, a language spoken on the island of Bougainville, Papua New Guinea, has only 12 letters in its entire alphabet—they are A, E, G, I, K, O, P, R, S, T, U and V.

**boy power** China has 32 million more boys under the age of 20 than it has girls.

**lonely lighthouse** The Stannard Rock lighthouse, Michigan, is the only structure on a large rock 23 mi (37 km) off the coast of Lake Superior. It was staffed for eight decades, until it was finally automated in 1962.

**ooh-la-law!** In 2010, French politicians finally sought to repeal a 1799 law that banned women in Paris from wearing pants except when riding horses or bicycles.

**new ring** In 2009, U.S. astronomers discovered a new ring around Saturn that is so large it could hold a billion Earths. The ring is made up of debris from Saturn's distant moon Phoebe.

**flood terror** In January 2011, torrential rain in the state of Victoria, Australia, killed over 22,000 sheep and 300,000 poultry and led to the formation of an inland lake of floodwater more than 50 mi (80 km) long. Farther north in Queensland, the floods submerged an area of land the size of France and Germany combined.

**the twitchhiker** Paul Smith traveled around the world for free in 30 days relying solely on the goodwill of people using the social networking site Twitter. By accepting free accommodation and transport from his fellow tweeters, he managed to travel from his home in Newcastle upon Tyne, England, to Stewart Island, New Zealand, via Amsterdam, Paris, Frankfurt, New York, Washington, D.C., Chicago, San Francisco, Los Angeles, and Auckland.

**deadly storm** On April 30, 1888, a violent hailstorm dropped ice balls the size of oranges on the city of Moradabad in India, killing 230 people.

# Ripley's crazy world
## Believe It or Not!®

**hamster hotel** In 2009, a hotel in Nantes, France, offered guests the chance to live like a hamster for a day. Architects Frederic Tabary and Yann Falquerho designed the room to resemble the inside of a hamster's cage, and for $130 a night visitors could feast on hamster grain, get a workout by running in a giant hamster wheel, and sleep in piles of hay.

**toilet tour** German guide Anna Haase runs a different kind of sightseeing tour—instead of showing visitors the traditional sights of Berlin, she takes them on a tour of the city's famous toilets. These range from a historic 19th-century toilet block to a Japanese automatic toilet that costs as much as a small car.

**tar lake** Covering an area of 100 acres (40 ha) and delving to about 250 ft (80 m) deep at the center, Pitch Lake on the island of Trinidad is filled with liquid asphalt, the result of oil being forced up through the faults on which the lake sits. Despite the highly toxic chemicals, the lake is home to bacterial life.

**tunnel network** During the Vietnam War (1955–75), Viet Cong soldiers using only hand tools dug a single tunnel network all the way from Saigon to the Cambodian border—a distance of over 150 mi (240 km). They created an underground city with living areas, kitchens, weapons factories, and field hospitals, installing large air vents (which were disguised as anthills or termite mounds), baffled vents to dissipate cooking smells, and lethal booby traps. Up to 10,000 people lived underground for years, getting married, giving birth, and only coming out at night to tend to their crops under cover of darkness.

**jesus image** While looking for holiday destinations on the mapping website Google Earth, Zach Evans from Southampton, England, spotted an outline of the face of Jesus Christ in satellite pictures of a field near Puspokladany, Hungary.

**sewage symphony** A sewage plant near Berlin, Germany, is breaking down sludge more quickly by playing the music of Mozart to its microbes. The composer's classics are piped in to the plant around the clock via a series of speakers because the sonic patterns of the music help stimulate activity among the tiny organisms, speeding up the breakdown of waste.

**bone décor** The Sedlec Ossuary in Sedlec, Czech Republic, is a Roman Catholic chapel containing more than 40,000 human skeletons, the bones of which have been arranged to form the chapel's decorations and furnishings.

**cave man** After living in a 7-ft-wide (2.1-m) cave for 16 years, officials evicted Hilaire Purbrick of Brighton, England, in 2009 because his underground home lacked a second fire exit.

**no flow** When astronauts cry in space, their tears stay in a ball against their eyes until they are wiped away, because there is no gravity to make them fall naturally.

**tough tree** A Sabal palm tree with a 6-in-wide (15-cm) hole through its trunk has survived several hurricanes in Estero, Florida.

**great hedge** The Great Hedge of India was planted across the country by the British in the mid-19th century to prevent salt smuggling. It was a 2,000-mi-long (3,200-km) barrier of living impenetrable thorny hedge that was patrolled by up to 14,000 attendants.

**snowball payment** For hundreds of years, Scotland's Clan MacIntyre delivered a single snowball in the summer to Clan Campbell as part of a long-standing debt.

## WEEPING GLACIER

A human face, appearing to cry, appeared in a glacier in Svalbard, Norway, in 2009. As the ice cap melted, the water poured into the sea, eroding the ice and creating the mysterious shape.

Away from the more organized areas of the catacombs, bones lie scattered in forgotten tunnels.

# Secret City

**Believe it or not, hidden directly below the busy streets of Paris, France, there are countless secret tunnels and caverns, and millions of human bones.**

*The city expanded so quickly in the 18th century that cemeteries and mass graves were soon literally overflowing—it is said that the cellar walls of adjoining buildings would ooze with human remains, and disease was rife. To solve the problem, bodies were removed each night and buried in caves adjoining the Parisian sewers. These catacombs—or underground cemeteries—and the tunnels between them were recycled Roman stone quarries that stretched for 500 mi (805 km). It is thought that the bones of six million Parisians are piled up in the catacombs—over half the current live population. It is still possible to wander through the maze of passages that run 65 ft (20 m) below the city streets.*

• French resistance troops used the catacombs as a base during World War II, as did occupying German forces. The tunnels also served as air-raid shelters for Parisians seeking refuge from enemy bombing.

• In 1787, the future King Charles X of France held a party in a large cavern deep in the catacombs.

• A gang of thieves was arrested in the catacombs in 1905 after attempting to steal skulls and bones to sell to medical students.

• A team of experts constantly surveys hundreds of miles of the catacombs to prevent any of the caves collapsing, which would potentially cause parts of the city, lying directly above them, to fall into the ground.

• An escaped orangutan perished in the Paris underground tunnels over 200 years ago. Its skeleton is still kept on public display.

• In 1871, 100 rebel soldiers escaped into the catacombs. They got lost in the dark tunnels and were never seen again.

IN THE MEMORY OF PHILIBERT ASPAIRT
LOST IN THIS QUARRY ON NOVEMBER 3RD 1793
FOUND ELEVEN YEARS LATER AND BURIED AT
THE SAME PLACE ON APRIL 30TH 1804

## BURIED ALIVE

In 1793, Philibert Aspairt descended into the catacombs under the hospital where he worked, hoping to steal wine from cellars belonging to monks. His body was found 11 years later, only yards from an exit.

OSSEMENTS DU
CIMETIERE DES
INNOCENTS
DÉPOSÉS LE
2 JUILLET 1809

THE GATEWAY TO THE CATACOMBS STATES
*"ARRETE! C'EST ICI L'EMPIRE DE LA MORT"*
("STOP! HERE IS THE EMPIRE OF DEATH.")

**🄡 RIPLEY RESEARCH**

The Gobi Desert is expanding into China very rapidly, claiming an area of 3,860 sq mi (10,000 sq km) each year—that's almost four times the size of the state of Rhode Island. The desert is now less than 50 mi (80 km) from Beijing, China, where the largest sandstorms can dump hundreds of thousands of tons of sand on the city.

🄡 **monster star** Scientists from the University of Sheffield, England, have discovered a new star that weighs 265 times the mass of our Sun and is almost 10 million times brighter. The monster star—named R136a1—is believed to be around a million years old and is so bright that if it were located where our Sun is, it would completely fry the Earth within minutes.

🄡 **disappearing island** An island that was at the center of a 30-year dispute between India and Bangladesh disappeared beneath rising seas in 2010. Measuring 2.2 mi (3.5 km) long and 1.9 mi (3 km) wide, uninhabited New Moore Island in the Bay of Bengal had been claimed by both countries—however, environmental experts said that global warming had finally resolved the matter of ownership.

🄡 *Snow Patrol* **To prevent bad weather spoiling important Moscow holidays, such as Victory Day and City Day, the Russian Air Force blasts snow clouds from the sky before they can reach the capital. When heavy snow is forecast for a Moscow celebration, airplanes spray liquid nitrogen, silver, or cement particles into the cloud mass, forcing the snow to fall on other parts of Russia instead.**

🄡 **painted peak** Using water jugs to splash an eco-friendly whitewash onto the rocks, a team of workers in Peru have painted the 15,600-ft-high (4,756-m) Chalon Sombrero mountain white. The peak in the Andes was once home to a sprawling glacier and it is hoped that the newly painted mountain will reflect away sunlight and help cool down the slopes to trigger a re-growth of its ice.

🄡 **meteorite attack** The same house in Gornji Lajici, Bosnia, was hit by meteorites six times in three years between 2007 and 2010. The repeated bombardment of white-hot rocks forced owner Radivoje Lajic to reinforce the roof with a steel girder. He says the chances of being hit by a meteorite once are so small that to be hit six times must mean that he is being targeted by aliens.

🄡 **windy planet** Wind speeds of 4,350 mph (7,000 km/h) were measured in 2010 in the atmosphere of planet HD209458b, which orbits a star in the constellation Pegasus, some 150 light years from Earth. The planet has a temperature of about 1,800°F (1,000°C) on its hot side.

🄡 **toxic island** Owing to the risk of toxic volcanic gases on Miyakejima Island, Japan, residents carry gas masks with them at all times—and sometimes even sleep with them.

🄡 **fish rain** For two days in February 2010, the remote desert town of Lajamanu in Australia's Northern Territory was bombarded with hundreds of small fish falling from rain clouds in the sky—even though it is 326 mi (525 km) from the nearest river.

🄡 **in the dark** A power outage in 2009 left the town of Quipeio, Angola (population 1,000), in the dark for more than two months.

🄡 **black gold** Beverly Hills High School in California has oil wells beneath its grounds, which earn the school hundreds of thousands of dollars in revenue every year.

# Sandstorm

*A vast sandstorm engulfed the town of Golmud in central China in May 2010 as it roared in from the Gobi Desert at a rate of 70 ft (20 m) a minute. Such storms are increasingly common in this area in springtime and, although often short-lived, they can cause electrical blackouts and induce breathing difficulties in residents.*

**glowing urine** A glowing trail spotted in the night sky above North America in September 2009 was caused by a falling block of astronaut urine. It came from the Space Shuttle *Discovery* which, unable to unload human waste while it was docked to the International Space Station, had then been forced to dump nearly two weeks' worth of waste in one drop.

**lightning hotspot** An area near the village of Kifuka, in the Democratic Republic of the Congo, has the greatest number of lightning strikes per square kilometer in the world—about 158 a year.

**deadly icicles** In the winter of 2009 to 2010, Russia's coldest in 30 years, five people were killed and over 150 injured by icicles falling from the rooftops of buildings in St. Petersburg.

**space smash** A 4.6-billion-year-old meteorite smashed through the windshield of a truck in Grimsby, Ontario, Canada, in September 2009. Minutes beforehand, local astronomers had witnessed a "brilliant fireball," 100 times brighter than a full moon, streaking across the night sky.

**starfish graveyard** More than 10,000 starfish died on a beach in Norfolk, England, in December 2009 after being washed ashore during a storm. The creatures had gathered in the shallows to feed on mussels, but were swept on to the beach during high tide and quickly perished once they were out of water.

**shrinking storm** Jupiter's giant storm, the Great Red Spot, shrank by more than 0.6 mi (1 km) per day between 1996 and 2006.

**high cloud** Morning Glory clouds, which appear regularly over Northern Australia each spring, stand one mile (1.6 km) high and can stretch for hundreds of miles. The clouds are often accompanied by sudden wind squalls and can move at speeds of up to 37 mph (60 km/h).

**rocky rain** On the distant planet COROT-7b, which is nearly twice the size of Earth, it rains rocks! Scientists from Washington University in St. Louis, Missouri, found that the planet's atmosphere is made up of vaporized rock, and when a weather front moves in, pebbles condense out of the air and rain down on the surface.

**bio blitz** On a single day in August 2009, a team of 125 scientists and volunteers found more than 1,100 species of life—plants, lichens, mushrooms, bees, bugs, butterflies, worms, and bats—in just 2 sq mi (5 sq km) of Yellowstone National Park, including several species not previously known to exist there.

**unconquered peak** Gangkhar Puensum, a mountain in Bhutan standing 24,836 ft (7,570 m) tall, is the highest unclimbed mountain on the planet.

**blown away** When Cyclone Olivia hit Australia's Barrow Island in 1996, it created a wind gust of 253 mph (407 km/h).

**changing places** The moons Janus and Epimetheus are in the same orbit around Saturn, with one a little farther out and slower than the other. The faster moon catches its neighbor every four years and the two moons swap places and the cycle begins again.

**single bloom** The *Tahina spectabilis* palm tree of Madagascar grows for decades up to a height of more than 50 ft (15 m) before it finally flowers for a single time, then dies.

▶ The building is designed to minimize twisting in high winds, but it still sways 5 ft (1.5 m) at its highest point. The 656-ft-high (200-m) spire was made from 4,000 tons of steel.

▶ The overall floor area of the building is 3,331,100 sq ft (309,469 sq m), the size of more than 700 basketball courts.

▶ The building is so large that it can take four months for a 30-strong team to clean the surface.

▶ Double-decker elevators ascend at an incredible 40 mph (64 km/h) to the 160th floor. Alternatively, there are 2,909 stairs from the bottom to the top.

▶ The glass on the Burj Khalifa would cover more than 30 football fields.

▶ The tower weighs 551,000 tons when empty. That's about the equivalent of 8,000 U.S. homes piled up on top of each other.

▶ At peak periods the tower uses enough electricity to power almost 20 passenger trains.

▶ Floors 77–108: Over 1,000 apartments. The tower is expected to hold 35,000 people at once—the equivalent of the population of a small town in one building.

▶ The building uses the weight of 26,000 family sedans in reinforced steel, and the exterior stainless-steel cladding weighs as much as 75 Statues of Liberty.

## Burj Khalifa

The Burj Khalifa, which opened in January 2010, is the tallest structure ever built. At 2,717 ft (828 m) tall, it is more than twice the height of the Empire State Building—the equivalent of 180 giraffes standing on each other's heads. Each of the 160 floors took just three days to build, with the complete tower taking 5½ years to finish, at a cost of $1.5 billion.

▶ In January 2010, two base jumpers made the highest ever free-fall leap from the 160th floor of the towers, free-falling for 10 seconds before opening their parachutes.

▶ 11,653,840 cubic ft (330,000 cubic m) of concrete were used in the construction of the tower. This is enough to have laid a sidewalk from London to Madrid—a distance of 785 mi (1,263 km).

▶ From the outdoor observation deck on the 124th floor, 1,483 ft (452 m) up, you can see Iran, 50 mi (80 km) away.

▶ Owing to Dubai's desert location, the Burj Khalifa is built to withstand sandstorms and temperatures of up to 118°F (48°C). The building moves up to 3 ft (1 m) as the metal expands in the heat. A water system collects enough condensation from the air conditioning every year to fill 20 Olympic swimming pools.

▶ There is an outside swimming pool on the 76th floor.

The Burj Khalifa is built on desert sand, so the tower's foundations are an incredible 165 ft (50 m) deep, filled with 110,000 tons of concrete. However, by the time of the official opening, the building had already sunk 2.5 in (6.3 cm) into the ground.

### happy harry
Harry Hallowes, an Irish tramp who squatted for more than 20 years in one of London's most expensive suburbs, was awarded a plot of land that could be worth up to $6 million. He was given squatters' rights to a patch of land 120 x 60 ft (36 x 18 m) on Hampstead Heath, where he has lived in a tiny shack since 1986.

### 4,200 clocks
The Pentagon, headquarters for the U.S. Department of Defense, has 4,200 wall clocks. Over 200,000 telephone calls are made from the Pentagon every day through phones connected by 100,000 mi (160,000 km) of cable, and although there are 17½ mi (28 km) of corridors, it takes only seven minutes to walk between any two points in the building.

### pub crawl
Rather than demolish the 124-year-old Birdcage Tavern to make way for a new road tunnel in Auckland, New Zealand, the country's transport authority decided to move the landmark hostelry 130 ft (40 m) up a hill. After the walls were reinforced by inserting carbon-fiber rods, the three-story building was jacked onto concrete rails lubricated with Teflon and liquid silicon, then painstakingly pushed up the hill by hydraulic ramps. The move took two days.

### gold machine
The Emirates Palace Hotel in Abu Dhabi, U.A.E., has a vending machine that dispenses gold bars—with prices updated to correspond to the world markets every 10 minutes.

### rat free
A Japanese shipwreck in 1780 inadvertently introduced rats to Rat Island, Alaska, and the island was heavily infested until 2009, when it finally became free of rats again—229 years later.

## BEER CRATE HOUSE
Architect Jörn Bihain used 43,000 plastic beer crates to create what he named the "Pavilion of Temporary Happiness," in the grounds of the Atomium building in Brussels, Belgium, in 2008. The vast temporary structure commemorated 50 years since the Atomium was erected at the 1958 Brussels World Fair.

### tower highway
The 16-story Gate Tower Building in Osaka, Japan, has a highway running through its middle between the fifth and seventh floors. An exit of the Hanshin Expressway passes through as a bridge, held up by supports next to the building. The office block's elevator moves through the vacant floors without stopping between floor four and floor eight.

### time for change
A giant astronomical clock at Wells Cathedral in Somerset, England, was painstakingly wound by hand for more than 600 years—and from 1919 to 2010 it was operated by five generations of the Fisher family. From 1987, Paul Fisher spent an hour, three times a week, turning the three 550-lb (250-kg) weights about 800 times. The weights were winched up on a pulley system and powered the clock as they descended over the next two days.

### gladiator school
The University of Regensburg, Germany, has a summer camp in which students live and train like Roman gladiators.

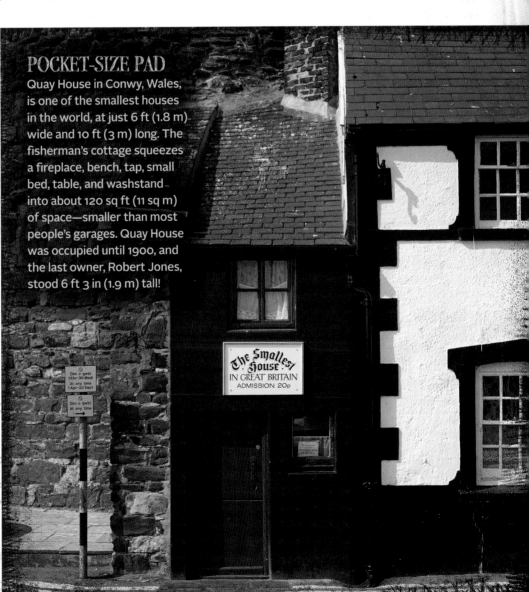

## POCKET-SIZE PAD
Quay House in Conwy, Wales, is one of the smallest houses in the world, at just 6 ft (1.8 m) wide and 10 ft (3 m) long. The fisherman's cottage squeezes a fireplace, bench, tap, small bed, table, and washstand into about 120 sq ft (11 sq m) of space—smaller than most people's garages. Quay House was occupied until 1900, and the last owner, Robert Jones, stood 6 ft 3 in (1.9 m) tall!

# Ripley's Believe It or Not!® index

# Ripley's
## Believe It or Not!®

## ACKNOWLEDGMENTS

COVER (t/l) Alain Van de Maele, (b/l) Malcolm Teasdale/KiwiRail, (r) Dmitry Dudin; 4 Photo by Havel Ruck Projects, "Inversion". 2005, (demolished), Dan Havel & Dean Ruck, Site-specific sculptural installation, Art League Houston, Houston, Texas; 6 (B) J.D. Griggs/US Geological Survey/Rex Features, (T) David Jordan/AP/Press Association Images; 7 (c/l) Ethel Davies/Robert Harding/Rex Features, (b) EPA/Photoshot; 8 (t) Donna Garde, TPWD, (b/r) John Terning, (b/l) Carl McCabe; 9 LatinContent/Getty Images; 10 (t, r) Jay Fine/Caters News; 10–11 (dps) Massimo Brega, The Lighthouse/Science Photo Library; 11 (b) Apex; 12 www.Freitag.ch; 13 (t) Photo by Havel Ruck Projects, "Inversion". 2005, (demolished), Dan Havel & Dean Ruck, Site-specific sculptural installation, Art League Houston, Houston, Texas, (b) Imagine China; 14 (t) Tsuzuki Minako, (b) Reuters; 15 Dmitry Dudin; 16 © Swim Ink 2, LLC/Corbis; 17 (l) © Rykoff Collection/Corbis, (r) © Blue Lantern Studio/Corbis; 20–23 (bkgd) Library of Congress; 24 (t/l, t/r) Solent News/Rex Features; 24 EPA/Photoshot; 25 © Hulton-Deutsch Collection/Corbis; 26 (t) © Russ Glasson/Barcroft USA, (c) © Vladone/istockphoto.com, (b) Malcolm Teasdale/KiwiRail; 27 (l) Mark Duncan/AP/Press Association Images, (r) U.S. Coast Guard photo by Petty Officer 2nd Class Lauren Jorgensen; 28 Specialist Stock/Barcroft Media Ltd; 29 Will Hunt; 30–31 ChinaFotoPress/Photocome/Press Association Images; 32 Bloomberg via Getty Images; 33 (t/l) Alain Van de Maele , (b) Tom Mackie/Photolibrary; BACK COVER Alain Van de Maele

Key: t = top, b = bottom, c = center, l = left, r = right, sp = single page, dp = double page

All other photos are from Ripley Entertainment Inc.
Every attempt has been made to acknowledge correctly and contact copyright holders and we apologize in advance for any unintentional errors or omissions, which will be corrected in future editions.